Raintree • Chicago, Illinois

FAMILY SURVIVAL

by Jan Clark

Illustrated by Deborah Allwright

© 2005 Raintree
Published by Raintree, a division of Reed Elsevier Inc.
Chicago, Illinois

Customer Service 888-363-4266

Visit our website at www.raintreelibrary.com

Illustrated by Deborah Allwright
Packaged by Ticktock Media Ltd.
Designed by Robert Walster, BigBlu Design
Printed and bound in China, by South China Printing

09 08 07 06 05
10 9 8 7 6 5 4 3 2 1

Library of Congress Cataloging-in-Publication Data

Clark, Jan (Janet Catherine), 1938-
  Family survival / Jan Clark.
      p. cm. -- (Kids' guides)
  Includes bibliographical references and index.
  Contents: Parents -- Brothers and sisters -- Stepfamilies -- Talking it through -- What would you do?
  ISBN 1-4109-0569-1 (lib. bdg.)
  1. Child psychology--Juvenile literature. 2. Children--Family relationships--Juvenile literature. 3. Family--Psychological aspects--Juvenile literature. [1. Family. 2. Stepfamilies. 3. Interpersonal relations.] I. Title. II. Series: Kids' guides (Chicago, Ill.)
  HQ772.5.C53 2005
  646.7'8--dc22
                                    2003021985

Some words are shown in bold, **like this.** You can find out what they mean by looking in the glossary.

CONTENTS

Introduction 4

Let's Talk About...

Parents 6

Brothers and Sisters . . 8

Stepfamilies 10

True Stories

My Big Brother 12

My Parents Split Up . . . 16

The New Baby 20

My New Family 24

What Would You Do? . . . 28

Glossary 30

More Books to Read 31

Index 32

INTRODUCTION

This book is about families. Most families are made up of people related to each other who share a home. They all look after each other. The adults work to provide shelter, food, and clothes.

Families often enjoy activities together such as going to the park and to movies. Some families have many people in them and some have a few. Can you see a family like yours in these pictures?

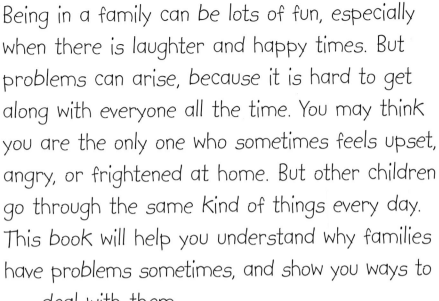

Being in a family can *be* lots of fun, especially when there is laughter and happy times. But problems can arise, because it is hard to get along with everyone all the time. You may think you are the only one who sometimes feels upset, angry, or frightened at home. But other children go through the *same* kind of things every day. *This* book will help you understand why families have problems sometimes, and show you ways to deal with them.

Let's Talk About...
PARENTS

Parents are people who are moms and dads. Children need at least one adult to take care of them as they grow from a baby into an adult. You may live with your real mom and dad, or your parents may have adopted you. You may live with only one parent because of a **divorce,** or your other parent may have died. You may also have **stepparents.**

BUT WHY ME?

Things might not always be very happy at home. If you are arguing with your parents, just remember that people do not always get along with one another all the time.

A parent's job is to guide you and help you to learn. They give you affection and praise when you do things right. They can get upset when you don't.

I asked Dad and he says I CAN go to the party!

Parents are pleased when you...

- clean your bedroom or look after your things.
- help out by feeding the family pet.
- are nice to your brother or sister.

Parents get angry when you...

- are naughty, demanding, shout, and slam doors.
- are mean to your brother or sister.
- have been told "No!" but go to the other parent, who says "Yes!" This makes them argue.

LOOK AT IT ANOTHER WAY

Even though moms and dads love their children, it's hard work being a parent. If they are on their own, have money worries, or have lots of children to feed and get dressed in the morning, they can get upset even though you have done nothing wrong.

Let's Talk About...

BROTHERS AND SISTERS

Brothers and sisters are **siblings** in a family with the same parents. Siblings may look similar, but they have their own likes and dislikes. They each need to feel special to their parents, so they feel loved.

Although most brothers and sisters love their siblings, they can annoy or get **jealous** of each other. They fight and compete when they are young, but often become **loyal** and **supportive** as they get older.

I told you not to play with my computer. Do it again and I'll tell Dad.

BUT WHY ME?

Quarrels between siblings are a fact of life, because all children want to do different things at different ages. If you are an only child, you may feel lonely at times and wish you had a brother or sister.

WHY DO I FEEL LIKE THIS?

It's normal to feel angry or frightened if your brother or sister hurts you. But being angry one day and friends the next happens a lot. An adult should be told if frightened, angry feelings happen very often.

It's my turn!

LOOK AT IT ANOTHER WAY

Brothers and sisters often think it's funny to tease or annoy each other. This is usually so they can get their own way or feel powerful. But it can cause very unhappy feelings, which you should talk about.

Rough-and-tumble games often begin in fun but can end in someone getting hurt. **Spiteful** words can hurt just as much. Yet some brothers and sisters enjoy fighting, even when one is younger than the other.

Here are some tips to stop things from always ending in a fight:
● Don't lose your cool. Take a deep breath and count to ten.
● Tell your brother or sister to stop or walk away. Don't hit each other.
● Try to remember that even though you may not want your sibling around now, you may become best friends one day.

Let's Talk About...
STEPFAMILIES

Stepfamilies are made if a mom or dad remarries. You may stay with both of your parents a lot, or you may not see one of them very often. Getting used to a **stepparent** and being part of a stepfamily can be a scary time. You may worry that your real parents won't love you as much when a stepparent becomes part of your life.

She always sides with her own kids.

BUT WHY ME?

If your parents split up, it's not your fault. It could happen to any child. It takes time to get used to being part of a stepfamily.

WHY DO I FEEL LIKE THIS?

Your unhappy feelings are caused by the change. You will feel better when things get settled. You may even be happier because your parents are happier. If you feel caught in the middle between your parents, tell them you just want to love them both.

It takes time to get used to being part of a stepfamily. You may find that you now have stepsisters or stepbrothers. You might have to share your bedroom. You might not like being told what to do by a stepparent. It's easy to argue, to hate them, and wish they'd go away. But learning to live together as a family means:

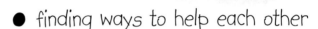

I don't want to share my room.

11

- saying sorry for mistakes
- talking about feelings
- finding ways to help each other
- not blaming each other when things go wrong.

Mom's looked sad ever since Dad died. It's good to see her happy again.

LOOK AT IT ANOTHER WAY

It is difficult for everyone, not just you. If you give it a chance, a stepparent could bring something special into your life, like helping to choose clothes, lending a hand with homework, or knowing lots about a favorite sport. A stepbrother or stepsister may turn into a great friend.

True Stories

MY BIG BROTHER

Hi, my name is Danny and I am eight years old. I live with my mom and dad, my older sister Lucy, and my brother Josh, who's twelve. Josh and I were at the same school until this year when he went to the big school. Now I don't see much of him. When he is home, he won't play with me.

Do you want to play?

Going to the mall. Sorry.

He doesn't even take much notice of his dog, Ruffles. Before, the three of us used to go to the park on Saturday mornings to play soccer. Ruffles is a really great goalie!

Yesterday Danny told us he had been chosen for his school's soccer team. He will have practice every Saturday morning now. Mom and Dad are proud of him. I said "Good job!" to Josh, but inside I don't feel happy. Saturdays won't be the same without him. It's not fair. Ruffles and I will miss him.

MY BIG BROTHER

Talking It Through

It helps to talk to someone...

A PARENT

Danny told his Dad about being upset. Dad said he could understand why. He said Danny should be happy for Josh, though. He can find someone else to play with on Saturdays.

A BROTHER

Danny told Josh it wasn't fair to Ruffles, since he would still need his exercise. Josh said sorry, but this was his big chance. He asked Danny to play with Ruffles on Saturdays. He promised to play with both of them at other times.

A COUSIN

Danny's cousin, Paul, said that the same thing happened to him when his brother joined a team. Paul felt left out and really missed his brother. But he's now the star of his own school team, and his brother is really proud of him!

FORWARD STEPS

- **TALK**
Don't keep your feelings bottled up.

- **CHANGE CAN BE GOOD**
It might mean new friends and more choices.

I took Dad's advice and talked to a new boy in our class who is crazy about soccer. His name is Alex. He and his family have just moved into a house on our street. I like him a lot.

Alex hasn't got any brothers or sisters, but he has a dog named Sam. They came over on Saturday, and we went to the park with Ruffles. Both dogs chased the ball around the field. Ruffles is a better goalie than Sam, because he jumps higher to catch the ball. When Josh came home from practice, he joined us, too. It was so much fun!

Now I'm looking forward to next Saturday!

True Stories
MY PARENTS SPLIT UP

16

Hi, I'm Kimberly. I'm seven years old and I live with my mom and my little sister, Susie. Dad did live with us, but he and Mom had really bad arguments. We couldn't get away from their shouting. And then one day Dad left. Mom cried and said he was never coming back to live with us. They were going to get a **divorce**.

Maybe it's my fault. I shouldn't have made Dad angry.

I don't want to move if I can't take Snowy.

Your rabbit is the least of my problems!

To make matters worse, Mom said we would have to move to a smaller house or an apartment. I might have to change schools. I'm worried about my rabbit. Mom got angry with me when I mentioned him.

It's so **confusing.** Dad has left, but Mom says he still loves me. I want him to come back and for things to be normal again, even with the shouting.

MY PARENTS SPLIT UP

Talking It Through

It helps to talk to someone...

A FRIEND

Anna offered to look after Snowy if Kimberly was unable to keep him. She could see him whenever she wanted. Anna suggested that Kimberly come around to play because her mom was good to talk to, if Kimberly wanted.

A GRANDPARENT

Kimberly's grandma suggested that they help her mom together. Kimberly can help with Susie, while Grandma helps Mom try to find a new home near Kimberly's school.

A TEACHER

Kimberly spoke to her teacher who said she was very sorry to hear the news. She suggested she talk about it in Circle Time the next day. Some of her classmates had been through the same thing.

FORWARD STEPS

- ### IT'S NOT YOUR FAULT
Your parents may not be able to live with each other any more, but they still love you.

- ### SHARE YOUR PROBLEMS
It can make you feel much better, and you might get some good advice, too!

I wish I saw my mom.

It's okay now.

At my school, we have Circle Time every Monday morning. We sit in a circle on the floor with our teacher. She asks if we have any problems.

I told my class what had happened, and noticed three others looking sad. One girl said she hadn't seen her dad for awhile, but now she sees him more often. Another said it was awful at first, but her parents get along okay now. One boy said he wished he saw his mom, since she had called him only twice since leaving home.

Everyone agreed it was sad when moms and dads split up, but that what happened afterward was different for everyone. I felt much better after talking at Circle Time.

We did move into an apartment, but I didn't have to change schools. Snowy is happy in his new home with Anna. I miss him and my dad, but I do get to see them a lot.

True Stories

THE NEW BABY

Hi, I'm Jade. I live with my mom and my stepdad, Dave. I was so excited when Mom and Dave told me they were expecting a baby. I would finally have someone to play with! I helped Mom choose the crib. We put it in my bedroom, with my favorite teddy bear. I hoped to have a sister named Barbie.

Then Mom told me it was twins, so I had to have another crib in my room and give away another teddy bear.

The trouble started after the twins, Angie and Keith, were born. Everyone says how cute they are and jokes about "double trouble." No one but me knows what that really means! They wake me up at night, hardly ever sleep, and they stink. Worse still, Mom is always tired. We never do things together anymore.

Why can't she send the babies back, then things would get back to normal?

Talking It Through

It helps to talk to someone...

A PARENT

Jade told Dave how tired of it she was. He said he knows it is hard for her now, but it will be fun once the twins get older. Then she will be able to play with them.

A GRANDPARENT

Jade talked to Nana who understood how much Jade was missing her mom. She suggested that Jade could help at feeding times. Nana said that she would come look after the twins so Jade and her mom could do something together.

A FRIEND

Jade told her friend Jackie, who said she was lucky to have a baby brother and sister. She said babies were so cute, and asked if she could come and see them.

FORWARD STEPS

● BE PATIENT

You will have fun times again very soon!

● THINK OF OTHERS

Try to think about how other people are feeling, too. Maybe you can be more helpful.

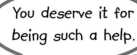
You deserve it for being such a help.

hanks, Mom!

I took Nana's advice and helped Mom at feeding times. I also help by putting away the twins' clothes and bottles. Mom says it is a big help knowing she can **rely** on me.

One morning, I realized the twins had not woken me up. They had slept all night!

The next Saturday, Dave went off to play baseball with his team, and Nana and Granddad took care of Keith and Angie. So I had Mom all to myself. We went shopping and she bought me a new ballet outfit, and we had ice cream in the park. When we got home, everyone was asleep. Granddad was snoring!

I look forward to teaching Angie ballet when she's old enough. She can have my outfit when I've grown out of it.

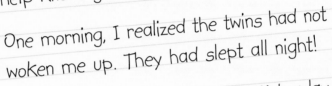

True Stories

MY NEW FAMILY

Hi, my name is Sarah. I'm eight years old and I live with my dad, my stepmom Julie, and her three children. Annie is thirteen, Jonathan is twelve, and Kate is the same age as me. Mom **divorced** Dad. I stay with her and her boyfriend every other weekend. Dad and I were on our own until he met Julie.

I like Julie but she is really **strict.** Mom lets me stay up until 9 P.M. but Julie says I should be in bed by 7.30, like Kate. That means I don't see my Dad, because he isn't back from work by then.

I don't want to go to bed yet.

The others are okay, but Annie thinks she is so grown up. She's always showing-off, trying on Julie's shoes and make-up. The worst thing, though, is that Dad and I used to go on bike rides together, but now Jonathan always comes. He rides ahead with Dad, and I'm left behind. It's not fair! I didn't ask them to come live with me.

MY NEW FAMILY

Talking It Through

It helps to talk to someone...

A PARENT

Sarah talked to her dad. He said Julie is in charge when he is not at home, but he will talk to her about bedtime. He said he wished he could get home earlier. He misses Sarah, too, when he doesn't see her.

A STEPBROTHER

Sarah talked to Jonathan about riding ahead with her dad. He said that he didn't realize she minded. He enjoyed going bicycling with both of them, and now he will ride behind sometimes.

A CLASSMATE

Sarah talked to Lorna, who has a stepfather. Lorna says it was horrible at first having to live with him and his three boys when she didn't even know them. Now it was okay. She said she would love to have a sister like Annie.

FORWARD STEPS

● **GIVE IT TIME**

You don't have to love everyone in your new family, but in time you may end up liking them.

● **BE HONEST**

People don't know how you feel unless you tell them.

Dad and Julie talked, and they agreed I could stay up two nights a week until he came home from work. We talk about our day, and sometimes he reads me a story. I have promised to go to bed at the same time as Kate for the other three nights.

I thought about what Lorna said and tried to spend more time with Annie. We tried on some of Julie's make-up together. We giggled so much!

Julie is not as **strict** now. And Jonathan showed me and Kate how to patch holes in our bike tires and fix the chain if it falls off. Now we all go on bike rides together. It is so cool!

Quiz

WHAT WOULD YOU DO?

1. What would you do if, like Kimberly, you were moving to a new house? Your Mom is worried about you and keeps asking how you feel.
a) Say you're fine (even if you're not). You don't want to worry her more.
b) Get angry.
c) Complain to friends.
d) Tell her how you're really feeling.

2. What would you do if your stepmom, like Sarah's, was more **strict** than your mom and you didn't like doing what she said?
a) Storm off and pout.
b) Yell, "You're not my mom, you can't tell me what to do!"
c) Talk to your dad about it.
d) Cry yourself to sleep.

3. What would you do if, like Danny, you were sad that your brother could no longer play with you?
a) Pretend it doesn't matter.
b) Secretly wish he'll get kicked off the team.
c) Tell him you're proud of him but you hope he can play with you sometimes.
d) Be angry and not talk to him.

4. What would you do if, like Jade, you were upset by the arrival of a baby in your family?

a) Say you're happy, even if you're not.
b) Start being naughty so that they have to notice you.
c) Be upset with the baby.
d) Talk to an adult about your angry feelings.

Answers

1. d) Putting a worried parent's feelings before your own won't help. A parent will feel better if you talk about what change really means to you.

2. c) Crying helps to let out the sad feelings you have, but it doesn't change things. Shouting just makes other people upset with you. Instead, talk about your unhappy feelings.

3. c) Ignoring your feelings won't make you feel better. Ignoring your brother will make you feel worse! But if you say good things, you will make your brother happy and you'll be praised when you do well.

4. d) Competing for attention with a baby won't take away your angry feelings. Tell an adult how you feel. He or she will help you find ways to feel better.

Glossary

confusing hard to understand

divorce married people who end their marriage get a divorce from a judge in court

jealous wanting to be like someone else or wanting to have something he or she has

loyal believe the best of someone even if they are unkind

quarrel argument or disagreement

rely trust someone will do what they promised

siblings brothers and sisters of the same family

spiteful behaving in a deliberately hurtful way

stepparent parent who is not the natural one by birth, but one by remarriage

strict following a fixed set of rules regardless of people's feelings

supportive when problems are heard with attention, or there is active encouragement of an activity

More Books to Read

Adams, Eric J. and Kathleen Adams. **On the Day His Daddy Left.** Morton Grove, Ill.: Whitman, 2003.

Bowen, Anne. M. **I Loved You Even Before You Were Born.** New York: HarperCollins, 2001.

Feeney, Kathy. **Feel Good.** Mankato, Minn.: Bridgestone, 2001.

Freeman, Martha. **The Trouble with Babies.** New York: Holiday House, 2002.

Maurer, Tracy. **A to Z of Friends and Family.** Vero Beach, Fl.: Rourke, 2001.

Powell, Jillian. **Family Breakup.** Chicago: Raintree, 1999.

Rotner, Shelley and Sheila M. Kelly. **Something's Different.** Brookfield, Conn.: Millbrook, 2002.

Index

adoption	6	only child	8
anger	5, 9, 17	parents	6–7, 10
arguments	5, 6, 7, 8, 9, 16	quarrels	8
brothers	7, 8–9, 12–15	saying sorry	11
death	6	sharing a bedroom	11, 20–21
divorce	6, 10, 16–19, 24	siblings	8–9
feeling left out	12–15	sisters	6, 8–9
fighting	8–9	stepfamilies	10–11, 24–27
happiness	5, 10, 11	stepparents	6, 10, 20
jealousy	8	teasing	9
new baby	20–23